*In everyone's life
there are moments
of pride and accomplishment
that are remembered forever...
Because you have been true to yourself
in the pursuit of your dream,
you have earned this moment
and the right to be proud of your
accomplishment.*

— Linda Principe

Be Proud
of All
You've Achieved

Reflections on the
Meaning of Success

A Blue Mountain Arts® Collection
Edited by Gary Morris

Blue Mountain Press™
Boulder, Colorado

Library of Congress Catalog Card Number: 94-1656
ISBN: 0-88396-374-4

ACKNOWLEDGMENTS appear on page 64.

Certain trademarks are used under license.

Manufactured in the United States of America.
Second printing of this edition: 2004

 This book is printed on recycled paper.

This book is printed on fine quality, laid embossed, 80 lb. paper. This paper has been specially produced to be acid free (neutral pH) and contains no groundwood or unbleached pulp. It conforms with all the requirements of the American National Standards Institute, Inc., so as to ensure that this book will last and be enjoyed by future generations.

Library of Congress Cataloging-in-Publication Data

Be proud of all you've achieved : reflections on the meaning of success : a Blue Mountain Arts Collection.
    p. cm.
ISBN 0-88396-374-4
1. Success—Poetry. 2. American poetry—20th century. I. Blue Mountain Arts (Firm)
PS595.S82B4 1994
811'.54080353—dc20

94-1656
CIP

Blue Mountain Arts, Inc.

P.O. Box 4549, Boulder, Colorado 80306

Contents

You Have a Lot to Be Proud Of!

You have so many things
*   to be proud of:*
the challenges that made you
*   stronger,*
your determination that has
*   remained steadfast,*
and your willingness to keep
*   on the path*
and give it your best.
You stayed with your dream;
you worked hard;
you never quit.
Now we all know
there's nothing you can't do!
Dreams really do have a way
*   of coming true,*
and you've proven it.
This is the moment you've worked for —
*   enjoy it!*
Then follow your heart
*   and all the golden opportunities*
*   still ahead of you.*

— Linda E. Knight

You've Learned to Never Let Go of Your Hopes and Dreams

Never let go of your hopes, dreams, and goals. Never lose faith in your power to make the world a better place.

Go forward with your shoulders back, your head high, and a smile. With your enthusiastic spirit, perseverance, and integrity of character, put your intelligence, talents, and passion into action.

Never let setbacks excuse you from trying again. It often takes many attempts to be a success. Never hold on to the old just because it is comfortable for you; never pursue the new just because you think it will bring you happiness. Incorporate into your life the best of the old, then stretch yourself with new ideas, people, and challenges.

Never let negative people influence you or direct what you do. Always face forward and see your whole life shining bright for you. Never let go of your character, ideals, or activism for the good of this world.

Never let go of the passions that inspire you, guide you, and always smile on you. These passions will lead you to reach your fullest potential. Hold on to them and they will keep you honest, caring, kind, and generous with the finest gifts your heart can give.

— *Jacqueline Schiff*

Be Proud of
All You've Achieved

Special moments in life
need to be recognized
    and acknowledged.
Your success
is truly a special time in your life
and in the lives of all those
who care about your happiness.

Your achievement symbolizes
a time of completion
and a time for new thoughts
toward the future.
It is a time to stop and realize
what it means to work hard
    for something
and to reach the goals
that you have set and believed in.
As an individual,
you can stand up and feel proud
of the independence and maturity
that have come from the dedication
and determination in your life.
You've earned your success,
and you should feel
so very confident within yourself
for all that you have achieved.

— Ben Daniels

Winners Are
People like You

Winners take chances.
Like everyone else, they fear failing,
but they refuse to let fear control them.

Winners don't give up.
When life gets rough, they hang in
until the going gets better.
Winners are flexible.
They realize there is more than one way
and are willing to try others.

Winners know they are not perfect.
They respect their weaknesses
while making the most of their strengths.
Winners fall, but they don't stay down.
They stubbornly refuse to let a fall
    keep them from climbing.

Winners don't blame
  fate for their failures
nor luck for their successes.
Winners accept responsibility
  for their lives.

Winners are positive thinkers
who see good in all things.
From the ordinary, they make
  the extraordinary.
Winners believe in the path they
  have chosen
even when it's hard,
even when others can't see
  where they are going.
Winners are patient.
They know a goal is only as worthy
as the effort that's required
  to achieve it.
Winners are people like you.
They make this world
a better place to be.

— *Nancye Sims*

*Success comes to those who are
willing to sacrifice
their immediate gratification
in order to achieve
long-term satisfaction.
You know what success means
because you have devoted yourself
to accomplishing the goals
you believe in.
You are someone who reaches out
for dreams
and continues to strive toward
finding new ones.*

*You are a success
and should feel so proud
of the motivation that you possess.
Keep believing in yourself,
and find happiness
in all the days ahead.*

— Laura Medley

I Believe You Can
Accomplish Anything
You Choose

If you could see through my eyes,
I wonder what you'd be feeling right now,
because I can see you standing
   as you really are —
powerful, sensitive, determined,
   and gracious.
I can see you achieving everything
   you choose to achieve.
I can see you being exactly
who and what you want to be.
Look through my eyes for an instant,
and you'll see yourself
conquering all limitations.
Look through my eyes,
and see who you really are
and what you are capable of.
You can accomplish anything —
   I know you can.

— Lea Marie Tomlyn

Always Keep Your Dreams Alive

Now is a time for you to
celebrate… the accomplishment
of a dream you have worked
so hard to realize. You have shown
so many people how special you are.

Now is the time to begin
to pursue the next path,
to reach out for the next star,
and to achieve the things
*   that are so important to you.*

Always keep
*   your dreams alive.*

And keep them coming true.

— Collin McCarty

People Who
Achieve Their Dreams:

They have confidence
    in themselves
They have a very strong sense
    of purpose
They never have excuses
    for not doing something
They always try their hardest
    for perfection
They never consider
    the idea of failing
They work extremely hard
    towards their goals
They know who they are
They understand their weaknesses
    as well as their strong points
They can accept and benefit
    from criticism
They know when to defend
    what they are doing
They are creative
They are not afraid to be
    a little different
in finding innovative solutions
    that will enable them
    to achieve their dreams

— Susan Polis Schutz

As You Strive
for Your Goals...

May your life always be filled
with the joy of friends and family,
and may each day bring you
the pleasures and deep rewards
of love and friendship.
May your heart always be at peace.
In unsteady and uncertain times,
may you always have something to
hold on to as a source of comfort
and peace in your thoughts,
your beliefs, and your life.
May your efforts
always be rewarded, and may you
experience the joy of achievement
and always have the excitement
of meaningful challenges.

May you always find
the things that most matter to you;
may your responsibilities
still leave you with
the time and freedom for
the people and activities
that provide your deepest satisfaction.
May the end of every journey
provide a chance for reflection
and appreciation for everyone
who helped you
and for everything you gained
along the way.
May you always have reasons
   for giving thanks.

— *Garry LaFollette*

How to <u>Really</u> Celebrate Your Achievement

Live it up ✍ *Do something wild and outrageous that may take years to live down* ✍ *Congratulate yourself — there are some people who truly do get better and better, and one of them is definitely you* ✍ *Do something meaningful for yourself* ✍ *Remember that you deserve it* ✍ *Put any difficulties behind you* ✍ *Put your highest hopes and your secret dreams ahead of you* ✍ *Pursue them* ✍ *Continue to share all the wonderful things about you with all those who count on you to make the world so much brighter* ✍ *Smile* ✍ *Keep smiling* ✍ *Keep doing all the things you do so well* ✍ *Make a wish and make it come true* ✍ *And remember that so many people will be smiling and hoping and wishing and celebrating right along with you* ✍

— Chris Gallatin

You Stand on
the Summit
of Your Hopes

This is one of those rare moments in life when you find yourself looking back on where you have been, while at the same time looking forward to the future.

Behind you are precious memories of experiences that you will never forget, heartfelt emotions that will fade but never disappear, and ideals that will change in form but remain in substance.

Ahead of you are new challenges and goals. They may seem mere shadows today, but they will one day be central to your life.

It seems such a paradox to look backward and forward at once, but the significance of any achievement exists in that very contradiction. Without your past, you have nothing on which to build your future. Without the future, your past would have no opportunity to come into full bloom.

— Pamela Koehlinger

You Amaze Me Sometimes

You have so much talent
and so many gifts,
and you are always busy
doing something creative
and worthwhile.

Yet you give yourself
so little credit,
refusing to accept yourself
for what you are — a marvel.

So, I'll just say it for you...

"You are a very talented,
very gifted,
absolutely amazing
person!"

— Barbara J. Hall

What Is <u>Real</u> Success?

Everyone wants success, and yet they often don't know when they have it.

For most, it is the maddening chase toward a better way of life or more of something. More fame, power, recognition, money, or

material stuff.

For some, it is the understanding of a loving partner, the love of their child, or the people that they can count on when life throws them a curve.

I am coming to believe that success is not more material wealth, but peace, happiness, contentment, and love.

Most of all love.

Real success is not to be sought after in the outer world, but discovered in your inner world. I am not condemning the stuff of life. We all want the things that life offers.

But we don't need as much

as we think we do. Sooner or later you will discover that real success is to be found in loving relationships. With your family, friends, strangers, and anyone who crosses your path. It is kindness shared, support given and received, listening, giving, and caring.

These will endure while your car rusts, your toys break, and you tire of the temporary gratifications that bring you what you think is real.

What matters is people. What lasts is love. What counts are true friends, and if you treasure these you can count yourself a success.

— Tim Connor

You Did It!

You deserve to be credited
for defying the opinions
and expectations
of many of the people around you.
When they said
that it couldn't be done,
you would not hear.
You set your goals on something
that only you seemed to see,
and you refused to back down
until your dream was realized.

The course you chose
was demanding and difficult.
I saw you in the middle of situations
that required both courage and sacrifice
in order to achieve the greater end.
The scars you've earned are really
the marks of a true hero,
and I want to let you know
how proud I am to know you.

Seeing you set your goal
and gather the courage it took
to face the disbelief of others,
to struggle and forge your way
    to a new horizon,
has been an inspiration to me.
Your growth has helped me
to face my own challenges.

Thank you for showing those around you
    how not to ever let go.

— Rita J. Henins

The Will to Win

If you want a thing bad enough
To go out and fight for it,
Work day and night for it,
Give up your time and your peace and
*   your sleep for it,*
If only desire of it
Makes you quite mad enough
Never to tire of it,
Makes you hold all other things tawdry and
*   cheap for it,*
If life seems all empty and useless without it
And all that you scheme and you dream
*   is about it,*
If gladly you'll sweat for it,
Fret for it,
Plan for it,
Lose all your terror of God or man for it,

If you'll simply go after that thing that
  you want
With all your capacity,
Strength, and sagacity,
Faith, hope, and confidence,
  stern pertinacity,
If neither cold poverty, famished and gaunt,
Nor sickness nor pain
Of body and brain
Can turn you away from the thing that
  you want,
If dogged and grim you besiege and beset it,
  You'll get it.

— Berton Braley

Lose/Win

I have known the pain of
failure
frustration
disappointment
defeat

Because I have taken a chance on
winning
succeeding
achieving

It takes a lot of the first
to get some of the second

— *Natasha Josefowitz*

Knowing How to Overcome Failure Is Part of Being Successful

"Failure."
It's only a word.
But it carries with it so much pain
and so little concern,
so much frustration
and so little respect,
so much stress and so little
understanding
that people spend their lives
running through their days
in the hope of avoiding the long arm
of this little word.

To test your vision, you must risk
failure.

To temper your ego, you must attempt
the impossible.

To tell your story, you must
take a chance.

To see beyond the horizon, you must
spread your wings.

To be all you can be, you must
stretch, flex, try, and go beyond
your proven limits.

To bridge the silence, you must risk
rejection.

To advance into the unknown, you must
risk the peril of all your
previous beliefs and emotions
that feel so secure.

Failure is not negative. It is a teacher.
It molds, refines, and polishes you
so that one day your light will
shine for all to see.

It isn't the failure you experience
that will determine your destiny,
but your next step and then the next
that will tell
the story of your life.

— *Tim Connor*

On This Foundation, Build Your Future

Go forward with new dreams;
let their power lead you on.
Grow and learn as you go,
and never stop believing.
Move ahead with confidence,
always reaching forward.
The opportunities awaiting you are endless;
enjoy them as they unfold.
Find your place in the world,
and let your own star shine bright.
Never give up; always press on.
Each day is a fresh place to begin.
Get behind what you believe,
open your soul, and honor your dreams.
Celebrate who you are, all that you've done,
and all you've yet to accomplish.
Go for it!
May your future be bright
    with happiness and success.

— Linda E. Knight

The Meaning of Success

Success is being true to yourself: discovering what makes you happy, and going after it. It is not just dreaming, but daring to make those dreams come true.

Success is being satisfied with who you are and making the most out of yourself. It is being the best that you can possibly be.

Success is not just waiting for things to come to you, but making the most of the opportunities that you have. It is working hard and being committed to the task at hand.

Success is not just doing something, but doing it right. It is giving all that you can possibly give and becoming a better person for your efforts.

Success is taking chances. It is testing your abilities, pushing yourself to the limit, and going to places where you've never been before.

Success is knowing that you can't always win. It is losing with dignity and knowing that if you have done the best that you can do and learned from your mistakes, then you have indeed succeeded.

— Caroline Kent

SOME SECRETS OF SUCCESS...

To accomplish great things
we must not only act but also dream,
not only plan but also believe.

— Anatole France

The important thing
is this:
to be able at any
moment to sacrifice
what we are
for what we could become.

— Charles Du Bois

There is only one success —
to be able to spend your life
in your own way.

— *Christopher Morley*

No bird soars too high,
if he soars with his own wings.

— *William Blake*

When you do the common things in life
in an uncommon way, you will command
the attention of the world.

— *George Washington Carver*

You Can Change the World

Before you lies a journey we all must travel. A journey whose length is not as important as the footprints you will leave behind for others to follow. A journey that has many paths, and the one that you choose will decide the course your life will take. You can opt for the easy and well-trodden road, or you can venture down the one rarely traveled. Either way, you have the ability to make an impact upon this world, so long as you follow the leanings of your own heart rather than the desires of others. And whichever road you choose to walk, let it show that a good and noble person passed this way. One who never sacrificed convictions for a place in the sun or the easy gain, but one who kept to the true and right path. And let it also show that you did not count your wealth in riches, but in how many walk this earth with humanity in their hearts, because the footprints you made in this life showed you walked in the footsteps of love.

— Daniel Haughian

Nothing Can Stop a Dreamer

*A dreamer goes where
others do not dare
and sees beyond the ordinary,
moving with unlimited vision
and purpose.*

*A dreamer does not pause to worry,
will not hesitate along the way,
is not afraid of a challenge,
and does not despair
or become disillusioned.*

From a dreamer's eye,
  the view is breathtaking,
    the ideas are endless,
      and the possibilities
        go on and on.

A dreamer is blessed with
  enough imagination to see
    what life might hold,
  enough initiative to go after it,
    and enough inspiration and insight
      to succeed.

A dreamer can see far beyond today,
  into a future bright with promise.
A dreamer's dreams never end,
  until all those dreams come true.

— *Barbara J. Hall*

Special Wishes for You...

For every dream in your heart,
I wish you greater inspiration.

For every hope you seek,
I wish you unexpected miracles.

For every opportunity awaiting you,
I wish you an extra chance.

For every challenge you meet,
I wish you a piece of your destiny.

Your greatest aspiration is but the
beginning of all that you have to offer.

So reach beyond yourself...
and let your heart carry you even higher.

— Barbara Vecqueray

Now That You've Reached This Goal...

The time has come for you
to take the path toward adventure
and the beginning of a new life.
As you reflect on your accomplishment,
let your mind think back
and remember the challenges
that you have faced and overcome,
the experiences that you have changed
into special moments.

After the congratulations
    and the celebrations,
you will be able to look
    to the future
and hold your head up.
You will come across many obstacles,
but you have your confidence,
    your courage,
        and your own belief in yourself
to overcome any boundary
that stands in your way.

— Veronica L. Kagawan

You Are an Inspiration

You are someone who inspires
the people around you
by the way you live your life
and the way you treat others.
You are focused on your future
and willing to give all that you are
to make your dreams come true.
You are always encouraging others
and supporting them
with your strong beliefs.
You are a motivated person
who takes chances when
they present themselves.
You never wait or worry about tomorrow;
you just keep focused on
what's happening today.
You are someone
who looks forward
to challenges
and fully accepts
both the joys and struggles
that come to you when life changes.

— Laura Medley

Keep Growing
and Learning

May you celebrate this accomplishment
within your heart.
May it be a steppingstone to
you, one that will lead to
new goals you want to reach.
May you never stop growing and
never stop learning, and may
a belief in yourself always
make a beautiful difference
in your days.
May you find that the world
encourages you to become all that
you are capable of becoming.
May every memory of your
yesterdays be filled with
feelings of warmth.
May friendships made in years
gone by grow and gain in all
the years ahead.
May the promise that lies before you
open wide its doors.

— Collin McCarty

This Is Just the First
of Many Dreams
That Will Come True for You

In the years ahead
I will look forward
to hearing about your accomplishments
and proudly telling everyone
that I know you
You are a unique person
and only you can do whatever
it takes to follow your dreams

So let your spirit lead you
on a path of excitement
and fulfillment
And know that
because you are a
determined and talented person
any dream that you dream
can become a reality

— Susan Polis Schutz

May Your Future Hold Only Bright Tomorrows

Follow your heart;
never surrender your dreams.
Constantly work toward your goals.
Believe in yourself, and always be truthful.
Take time to enjoy life's pleasures.
Keep your mind open
to new experiences.
Think before acting,
but don't forget the joys of spontaneity.
Make your own decisions.
Look out for yourself, but remember
that you share this universe with others.

Look for the good in others —
everybody has their own song to sing.
Live each moment to the fullest,
for a moment too soon becomes
a memory.
Look for opportunities, not guarantees.
Hope for the best.
Give people a chance to love you,
for that is how you learn to love.
Live your life for yourself,
but always be considerate of others.
Believe in tomorrow, for it holds the key
to your continued success.

— *Melissa Ososki*

Measure Success in Your Own Way

Success means something different
to each one of us,
but it comes to those
who are willing to work hard
and who continue to be dedicated
to making their dreams come true.

Success means setting goals
and focusing yourself
in the right direction
in order to reach them.
It means believing in yourself
and constantly reminding yourself
that you are capable of achieving
your desires.

But most of all,
success is being who you are,
and feeling proud of yourself
for every task and challenge
that you face and conquer
along the way.

— Dena DiIaconi

May All Your Dreams Become a Reality

Dreams can come true
if you take the time to
think about what you want in life
Get to know yourself
Find out who you are
Choose your goals carefully
Be honest with yourself
Always believe in yourself
Find many interests and pursue them
Find out what is important to you
Find out what you are good at
Don't be afraid to make mistakes
Work hard to achieve successes
When things are not going right
don't give up — just try harder
Find courage inside of you to remain strong
Give yourself freedom to try out new things

Don't be so set in your ways that you can't grow
Always act in an ethical way
Laugh and have a good time
Form relationships with people you respect
Treat others as you want them to treat you
Be honest with people
Accept the truth
Speak the truth
Open yourself up to love
Don't be afraid to love
Remain close to your family
Take part in the beauty of nature
Be appreciative of all that you have
Help those less fortunate than you
Try to make other lives happy
Work towards peace in the world
Live life to the fullest
Create your own dreams
and I know that your dreams will become
*   a reality*

— Susan Polis Schutz

Look Upon
Your Achievements
with Pride

In everyone's life
there are moments
of pride and accomplishment
that are remembered forever.

Through the years,
you have set goals and met each challenge
with enough courage and determination
to overcome the many obstacles
that you've encountered along the way.

Success is not measured by how well
you fulfill the expectations of others,
but by how honestly you live up to
your own expectations.
Because you have been true to yourself
in the pursuit of your dream,
you have earned this moment
and the right to be proud of your
accomplishment.

— Linda Principe

Life Lessons to Always Remember

Remember that reaching your destination is only part of living. Enjoying the journey is the other.

Remember that no one person in life can make you happy. True happiness comes from within.

Remember that words are very powerful, and they stay around forever — so always make sure that what you say counts.

Remember that true love is the most precious gift of all and the most tender of all emotions. Be sure to give it out as much as possible.

Remember that no one has all the answers to life. Life is an adventure that must be enjoyed to the fullest. Sometimes it is the surprises along the way that make it all worthwhile.

Remember to be kind to the strangers you meet along your path. You never know how they might touch your life.

Remember that if today seems dark, tomorrow may be brighter. Sometimes we need to get lost in the darkness before we can fully appreciate the light on our path.

Remember to appreciate the moment you are in. When you live in the past or for the future, you miss everything in between, and you will have never truly lived.

Remember to take a new path home today. You may learn something new that will change you forever.

Remember that change is a good thing. When you learn new things and take on new challenges, you expand your mind and become a better person for it.

Remember that if you love someone, tell them. Life is short and it moves very quickly. Loving someone openly gives purpose and meaning to your days.

Remember to stop and take a breath. Life is not a race to be won. The only way to enjoy all of it is one moment at a time.

— Rebecca Finkelstein

The Key to Your Future
Is in Your Hands

You are the only one
with the power
to make your life
all that it can be.

There will be difficult challenges
    and changes to face.
But you're a courageous person,
and fear is such a small word that,
    once faced, will lose all its power
    to hold you back.

Just take each challenge
one step at a time,
    and refuse to give up.
Believe in yourself, and don't let
    the opinions of others
influence your actions
    or decisions.
You are the key to your future.
Make it the best it can be.

— Barbara Cage

ACKNOWLEDGMENTS

The following is a partial list of authors whom the publisher especially wishes to thank for permission to reprint their works.

Jacqueline Schiff for "You've Learned to Never Let Go of Your Hopes and Dreams." Copyright © 2003 by Jacqueline Schiff. All rights reserved.

Laura Medley for "Success comes to those who are willing..." and "You are someone who inspires...." Copyright © 1994 by Laura Medley. All rights reserved.

Barbara J. Hall for "You Amaze Me Sometimes" and "Nothing Can Stop a Dreamer." Copyright © 1994 by Barbara J. Hall. All rights reserved.

Tim Connor for "What Is _Real_ Success?" From WALK EASY WITH ME THROUGH LIFE by Tim Connor. Copyright © 1992 by Tim Connor. And for "Knowing How to Overcome Failure Is Part of Being Successful." Copyright © 1994 by Tim Connor. All rights reserved.

Rita J. Henins for "You Did It!" Copyright © 1994 by Rita J. Henins. All rights reserved.

Natasha Josefowitz for "Lose/Win." From NATASHA'S WORDS FOR LOVERS by Natasha Josefowitz, published by Warner Books. Copyright © 1986 by Natasha Josefowitz. All rights reserved.

Caroline Kent for "The Meaning of Success." Copyright © 1994 by Caroline Kent. All rights reserved.

Daniel Haughian for "You Can Change the World." Copyright © 1994 by Daniel Haughian. All rights reserved.

Barbara Vecqueray for "For every dream in your heart...." Copyright © 1994 by Barbara Vecqueray. All rights reserved.

Dena Dilaconi for "Success means something different...." Copyright © 1994 by Dena Dilaconi. All rights reserved.

Rebecca Finkelstein for "Life Lessons to Always Remember." Copyright © 2003 by Rebecca Finkelstein. All rights reserved.

Barbara Cage for "The Key to Your Future Is in Your Hands." Copyright © 2003 by Barbara Cage. All rights reserved.

A careful effort has been made to trace the ownership of poems used in this anthology in order to obtain permission to reprint copyrighted materials and give proper credit to the copyright owners. If any error or omission
has occurred, it is completely inadvertent, and we would like to make corrections in future editions provided that written notification is made to the publisher:

BLUE MOUNTAIN ARTS, INC., P.O. Box 4549, Boulder, Colorado 80306.